Giraffes

Leo Statts

abdopublishing.com

Published by Abdo Zoom™, PO Box 398166, Minneapolis, Minnesota 55439. Copyright © 2017 by
Abdo Consulting Group, Inc. International copyrights reserved in all countries. No part of this book may be
reproduced in any form without written permission from the publisher. Abdo Zoom™ is a trademark and logo
of Abdo Consulting Group, Inc.

Printed in the United States of America, North Mankato, Minnesota
062016
092016

Cover Photo: Shutterstock Images
Interior Photos: iStockphoto, 1, 9, 10, 15, 16; W. L. Davies/iStockphoto, 4–5, 12–13; Shutterstock Images, 6, 7,
17; Sherrod Photography/Shutterstock Images, 8; Red Line Editorial, 13, 20 (left), 20 (right), 21 (left), 21 (right);
Hazlan Abdul Hakim/iStockphoto, 14; Matt Abbe/iStockphoto, 18–19; Henk Bentiage/iStockphoto, 19

Editor: Emily Temple
Series Designer: Madeline Berger
Art Direction: Dorothy Toth

Publisher's Cataloging-in-Publication Data
Names: Statts, Leo, author.
Title: Giraffes / by Leo Statts.
Description: Minneapolis, MN : Abdo Zoom, [2017] | Series: Savanna animals |
    Includes bibliographical references and index.
Identifiers: LCCN 2016941162 | ISBN 9781680792010 (lib. bdg.) |
    ISBN 9781680793697 (ebook) | ISBN 9781680794588 (Read-to-me ebook)
Subjects: LCSH: Giraffes--Juvenile literature.
Classification: DDC 599.638--dc23
LC record available at http://lccn.loc.gov/2016941162

Table of Contents

Giraffes

Giraffes are tall **mammals**.

Their necks are long.
So are their legs.

Giraffes walk slowly.

They run fast. A giraffe can run up to 35 miles per hour (56 kmh).

Giraffes have large eyes and ears.

They have
two short
knobs on
their heads.

Their fur has brown spots.

Tan or white lines separate the spots. Each giraffe has a different pattern.

Habitat

Giraffes live in Africa.
They are found in dry, open areas.
Some live in **savannas**.
Others live in **woodlands**.

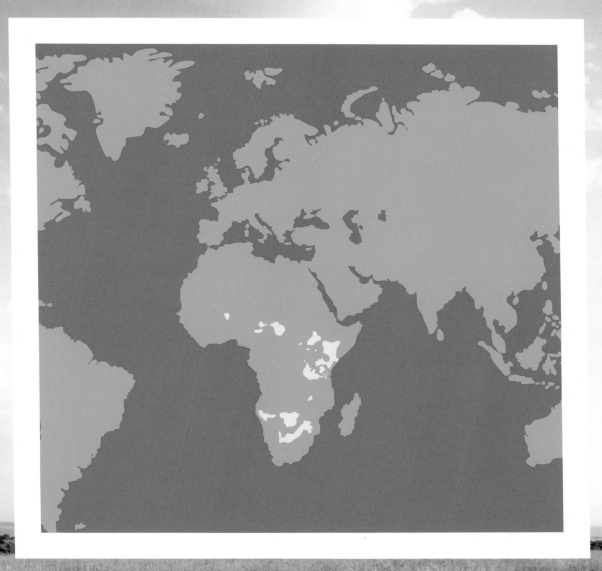

Where giraffes live

Food

Giraffes reach for food high in trees.

14

They eat leaves.
They eat twigs and fruit.

Giraffes have long tongues.
Their tongues are strong.

The tongues can grab
and hold objects.

Life Cycle

Giraffes live in **herds**.
A baby giraffe is called a **calf**.

Giraffes live on their own
after one or two years.
They can live up to 25 years.

Average Height

A giraffe is taller than a basketball hoop.

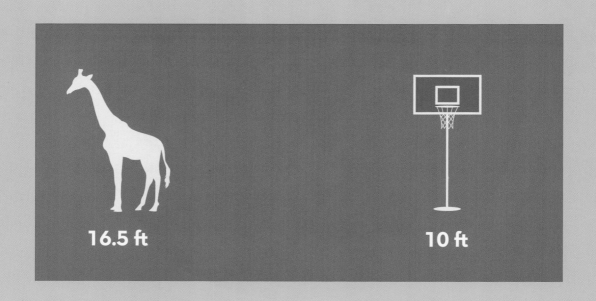

16.5 ft   10 ft

Average Weight

A giraffe is heavier than two soda vending machines.

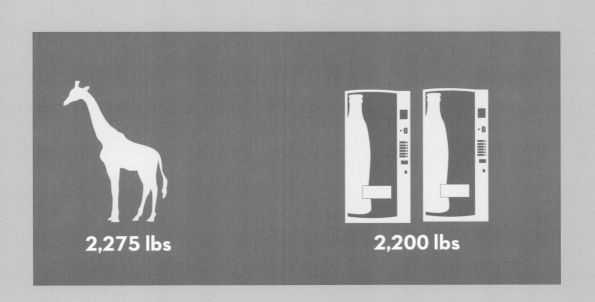

2,275 lbs   2,200 lbs

Glossary

calf - a baby animal.

herd - a group of animals.

mammal - an animal that makes milk to feed its young and usually has hair or fur.

pattern - a regular marking.

savanna - a grassland with few or no trees.

woodland - land covered by woods or trees.

Booklinks

For more information
on giraffes, please visit
booklinks.abdopublishing.com

Zoom In on Animals!

Learn even more with the Abdo Zoom
Animals database. Check out
abdozoom.com for more information.

Index